Blockchain

How the Technology Behind Bitcoin Is Changing Money and Business

By Mark Bresett

BONUS: DOWNLOAD MY
<u>FREE</u> BOOK

Thank you for purchasing my book.

I would like to offer you a FREE book *25 Ways to Build Wealth: Reach Your Ultimate Goal With These Smart, Simple Steps*.

To get this 100% free book, just visit my website:

www.Ways2BuildWealth.com/book

Table of Contents

Introduction

Congratulations on purchasing your personal copy of Blockchain: How the Technology Behind Bitcoin Is Changing Money and Business. Thank you for doing so.

The following chapters will discuss how the world is changing from a technological perspective. We will specifically be looking at the revolutionary technology behind the cybercurrency network known as blockchain. Perhaps you have heard of blockchain before, and perhaps you have not. Regardless, blockchain is certifiably changing the way that people interact with the world both financially and non-financially alike. If you're someone who likes to be up-to-date on all of the latest technological advancements in our society, then there is no doubt that this book is for you.

After reading this book, you will have discovered why the world needs the technology that blockchain can provide, as well as understand how this innovative technology works in detail. This will include a conversation on not only trust in the marketplace but also notions such as private and public keys, decentralized networks, cryptography, nonce numbers, and hash functions. These concepts may seem foreign to you now, but by the end of this book, you will have a vast understanding of each concept, as well as their importance.

The last chapter will discuss the long-term implications of blockchain and the future of this complicated yet highly important network system. As you will see through our discussion of the website Intrade.com in the first chapter, transparency is an issue that is highly important if a website wants to thrive in the cyber sphere. Blockchain is able to provide this transparency, along with other elements such as security and decentralization. With blockchain being able to achieve all of these concepts, there are many people who wonder about how our traditional organizations such as banks and the stock market will look in the future. If our society no longer needed physical buildings in order to function properly, what would our society look like? Blockchain is one of the first solid manifestations of a world where people can largely own currency and other types of products without physical paperwork, and the development of blockchain is exciting for a variety of reasons. You can rest assure that you will learn about all of these exciting reasons by reading this book.

There are plenty of books on this subject on the market. Thanks again for choosing this one! Every effort was made to ensure it is full of as much useful information as possible. Please enjoy!

Chapter 1
The Importance of Cyber Transparency in the Modern Age

It is relatively easy to agree on the fact that transparency in any marketplace is extremely important. If people don't feel as if they can trust the institution with whom they are spending their money, it is unlikely that a large number of people will continue to spend their money through these means for very long. In the physical realm, most people feel as if they can trust most of the places where they choose to spend their money. For example, when you go to the grocery store, it's likely that one of the last thoughts that you're having as you go to the checkout counter to pay for your goods is the idea that the grocery store is going to steal your money or trick you in some deceptive way. The same came to be said for many other places where you probably frequently shop, including the shopping mall, the drug store, or a fast food restaurant. A primary reason why you feel safe shopping in these places is because they've been around for a long time and many other people have been patrons at these places safely in the past. There is an element of familiarity with these places, and this keeps consumers coming back for more time and again.

Many of us will agree that the Internet is a different creature. There are online institutions that have been around for a long time, such as Amazon or eBay; however, there can sometimes be instances where we feel as if a transaction is going to go wrong or our information may be hacked in some frightening way. It doesn't help that there are plenty of stories out there about how smart hackers have swindled innocent Internet users out of their money through cyber tricks that no layman could possibly begin to understand. Of course, you bought this book thinking that it would not be about trust in the marketplace, but this is an extremely important aspect of why blockchain technology is relevant. As society develops to be more digitally savvy, trust in intangible goods such as currency is becoming increasingly important. Without a way to verifiably let consumers know that their transactions are safe, how will there ever be progress? The basic point here is that it is becoming increasingly clear that blockchain technology is able to bridge the gap between the consumer and the notion of trust and transparency within the digital marketplace.

A Quick Case Study: Intrade.com

To put the idea of trust that is currently lacking within the digital marketplace into perspective for you, we can use Intrade.com as an example. From its onset, the goal of Intrade.com was a place where people could go to predict the future on certain events in exchange for money. Some would say that this online forum was a place that was able to circumvent the illegal fees that are associated with gambling and predicting the future. The stock market is the equivalent of Intrade.com because every day professional brokers head to Wall Street in an attempt to win money with information that they are trying to predict about the future. The difference between Wall Street and Intrade.com is that Wall Street is regulated by the government, and there are also many regulations within the stock market itself that keeps the big players from completely dominating the market unfairly. With Intrade.com, this was not the case. With very little regulations in place, this digital prediction market could be considered "fast and loose" by many.

While the ins and outs of Intrade.com worked similarly to a stock market, a more colossal problem that this predictions platform and others like it faced revolved around the fact that there was no way to verify that physical money could back up the digital money that was being exchanged online. This is a primary reason why Intrade.com ended up shutting down. When people wanted to cash out, they were faced with the unfortunate reality that the online company could not pay them because these funds did not actually exist in real time. With no verification process within the online trading system, it has been proven time and again that the online trading system will fall apart and leave the people who have been using it left for broke.

Even though these systems do not work as they stand, the solution that has come to the forefront over the years is the blockchain system. As you will see as you read this book, a blockchain system is able to completely verify that funds do actually exist within a network. For this reason, today blockchain is highly regarded as possibly being able to change the way that the entire stock market works and how information is traded amongst people from the perspective of predictive gambling. Some people think that if blockchain is able to hold people more accountable for the predictions that they're making, this will help to make people more careful with the way that information is being exchanged because when someone predicts something wrongly, funds will be deducted from their digital account.

Digital forms of currency seem to be a natural progression that is coming from a sense that the future may exist within the digital realm rather than through the physical realm. Can you imagine how the world would look if we didn't need physical banking buildings anymore, or physical buildings for stock market transactions to take place? Blockchain could potentially completely change our physical infrastructure and the organization of our societies. Who knows, maybe one day we will have more physical space than we do now because less buildings will need to be created. If this does happen, it is safe to say that we will have blockchain technology to thank for this societal revolution.

Chapter 2

The Backbone of Bitcoin, Decentralization, and Public and Private Keys

This book is going to explain how blockchain methodology works through the cryptocurrency network known as bitcoin. Bitcoin is a type of cryptocurrency or digital currency. An individual user on the bitcoin network is able to decide how much his or her bitcoin currency is going to be worth and can divide 100,000,000 units of bitcoin as many times as he or she wishes in order to obtain their own unique bitcoin value. It's also important to note here that a "bitcoin" can be delineated into other types of currency, including a dollar, a yen, and so on. It can also represent a unit of energy, or even ownership in something. In this way, a bitcoin is concerned with maintaining an individual's ownership of something, as much as it is concerned with currency exchange. In order for these concepts to be protected, cryptographic methods have also been developed. These methods are able to serve as a security system for a blockchain network. Two main cryptographic methods that are used within a bitcoin system include the public key and private key. We will discuss both of these methods in this chapter.

Today, it is common knowledge that the blockchain system works better than does the bitcoin application on which it was initially developed. The question as to whether or not bitcoin has reached its peak as a viable online application is still open, yet blockchain is quickly becoming a highly dependable form of technology for the future. Some of the key concepts at which this chapter will look include the ideas of decentralization, cryptocurrency, and private and public keys. In seeking to gain a more intimate understanding of how blockchain got started and the breadth of decentralization, we will also briefly touch on the origin of bitcoin.

Decentralization and Transparency in a Previously Centralized World

As we saw in the previous chapter, the Internet is in need of more trust in their marketplace, but it can also be argued that Internet entities are not the only businesses that are in need of a trust revitalization. Another colossal entity that is need of more consumer trust are the banks. Without getting into too much detail, it's largely known that the 2008 economic crisis was primarily caused by banking corporations having selfish interests and not looking out for their customer's money. This notion is similar to the fraud that was seen in the example provided by the events surrounding intrade.com; however, the biggest difference that needs to be emphasized between these two entities is that one took money via the Internet and one took money via brick and mortar buildings.

Regardless of how the public was deceived, they were deceived nonetheless. The removal of a third-party entity such as a bank that is able to privately interfere with a consumer's money is the problem that blockchain can solve. By emphasizing the ideals of transparency and security simultaneously, blockchain is able to create an environment that is safe and accessible for anyone on the network at any given period of time. This is something that concrete banking institutions and online networks that do not use blockchain cannot guarantee or provide. This is why blockchain matters.

How Bitcoin Helped to Popularize the Concept of Decentralization

Prior to the development of bitcoin, anyone who was discontented with the feeling of distrust in the marketplace really had nowhere to turn. Bitcoin, and more specifically the blockchain technology that was running behind it, helped to change all of that. Bitcoin as a concept originated through a paper entitled "Bitcoin: A Peer-to-Peer Electronic Cash System". This paper was authored by a man who went by the last name Nakamoto; however, to this day, it cannot be determined whether or not this person actually exists. This paper was written in 2008, and in 2009, the first bitcoin transaction was initiated. Because of bitcoin's popularity, it may seem strange that the name who wrote the paper that led to its popularity seemed to disappear off the face of the earth, but this seems to be consistent with the notion of blockchain to begin with. This can best be explained through an explanation of what exactly was in Nakamoto's paper.

This paper "Bitcoin: A Peer-to-Peer Electronic Cash System" sought to explain the basics of what bitcoin currently stands for, which is a platform for automated cryptocurrency to be exchanged between two people digitally all without any third-party interference from a bank or money manager. Additionally, this paper also articulated the importance of the community of users within the bitcoin network all being responsible for being cognizant of all of the transactions that are taking place within the network during any given period of time. This way, every user within the network knows exactly what is going on within it, and maximum transparency is possible. This notion of transparency and decentralization through shared awareness and responsibility can possibly explain the mystery surrounding Nakamoto's identity. If there was a single person who was the "creator" of bitcoin, this would mean that it would be more likely that everyone would go to Nakamoto when decisions needed to be made about the network. Nakamoto's anonymity requires that everyone within the bitcoin network must share responsibility of the network itself, and this emphasizes the concepts of transparency and decentralization that the blockchain can offer its digital clients.

Public Keys and Private Keys: Two Pillars of Blockchain Security

It makes sense that in a completely decentralized system such as a blockchain, the encryption security system is also decentralized and maintained through the user interface. This is done via mechanisms that are known as private and public keys. These are cryptographic methods, and we will talk about the notion of cryptography in the next section. First, we will talk about public and private keys. If you've ever seen a pen and a pen cap, you can think of the public and private keys as working in a similar way. These keys work with one another within the blockchain network in order to secure transactions that occur between individuals on the network. Specifically, it's important to understand that every wallet that exists within the bitcoin network is given both a public and a private key. Let's talk about both of these key types because these keys are both extremely important aspects of how encryption operates on a blockchain network. Before we get into the details on these, it's also important to understand that in order for a transaction to be completed on a blockchain network, both the sender and the receiver must authorize any transaction. If this authorization does not occur, then it will not be completed.

The Basics of the Public Keys

You can think of the public key as being similar to a person's home address mailbox. A mailbox is able to receive messages that people who are living inside of a home can respond to if they wish. Obviously, the inside of the home is not accessible to anyone other than the homeowner, unless the homeowner allows an outside person access into the home. A blockchain network operates in a similar manner. Let's say that you yourself decide to open a bitcoin account. This means that you receive a wallet of your own and have your own public key. Once you have your wallet up and running, you start to receive requests to make transactions from other users on the bitcoin network. These users are sending their private key to your public key, in an attempt to prove to you that they have funds, which they claim they have. More information on this concept later. For now, all that is important is that you understand that the function of the public key is to provide a user with the ability to either approve or deny transactions from other users on the blockchain network.

The Basics of the Private Keys

Similar to the public key, every single wallet on the blockchain network has a private key. Except for the fact that every wallet contains both a private key and a public key, the private key can largely be considered to be the direct opposite of the public key. The private key is well... private; however, this key can be sent to other users on the network when an individual is looking to make a transaction with another individual on the network. For example, let's say that you want to send money to another bitcoin user. To do this, you would initiate the transaction by sending your private key to the individual's public key. Once this happens, it means that you are digitally agreeing to allow the individual at the other end of the transaction to see your private key and confirm the funds that are available in your account. In this way, it is easy to see how the private key and the public key work together.

The Notion of the Public Ledger

It's also important to understand the notion of a public ledger that exists within any blockchain network. The public ledger can be best described as a document that everyone on the blockchain network receives. This document is important in maintaining transparency within the blockchain network because it verifies that all of the transactions that are on the blockchain network make sense and that all of the available funds within a blockchain network add up to the correct amount. Thus, an individual is able to use the public ledger in conjunction with the public and private keys, and this ensures that both parties are acting in truthful and honest ways. The public key verifies that the funds are coming from a location that is publicly accessible on the bitcoin network, and the private key and public ledger reinforce that both parties have the funds that they say they do. These are the basic working pieces within a blockchain network that come together to maintain transparency. Without these elements, a blockchain network would be less safe. It's also important to understand that while we are talking about blockchain primarily from the perspective from bitcoin, a blockchain's public ledger could also be used to verify other types of transactions, such as to confirm ownerships of contracts or other types of intangible goods or services.

Sweeping

If you want to be up-to-date on the latest blockchain lingo, then it's important that you understand the concept of sweeping. We have already discussed sweeping without actually giving it a formal name. This is when an individual gives their private key to someone else in the blockchain network prior to a transaction taking place; however, there is another aspect to it that we have yet to discuss. Not only is it important to know that the private key verifies activity between individuals, but it is also important to understand that an added step of verification includes the idea that this activity is going to be documented and sent to everyone on the blockchain network. This means that if your name was Riley and you were to send your private key to someone named Trevor, everyone on the network would receive notification when you send your private key to Trevor. Again, this helps to make sure that both Riley and Trevor are not in cahoots with one another and that there is no thievery going on within the blockchain network.

Chapter 3
The Interaction Between Miners, Hash Functions, and Nonce Numbers

Even though bitcoin has always operated far better than sites such as Intrade.com, this is not to say that it did not have its own set of problems when it was first being developed. The basis of this problem was that bitcoin was having a difficult time putting its transactions in sequential order. On a small scale, it may seem like it would be easy to make sure that all of the transactions within a blockchain network could go into sequential order, but on a larger scale, this becomes a bigger problem. Let's say that you (Riley) completes a transaction with someone at 2:31 PM. There are a lot of other people on this network, and it is not far-fetched to think that two other people have also completed transactions at the exact same time as you and someone else. When this happens, a blockchain has to figure out which transaction is going to appear on the public ledger first.

The need for transactions to occur in sequential order is important for a blockchain network because of the fact that if people can't see where the money is going during a specific period of time, there is a greater chance that funds will get duplicated and people could end up stealing from others. Ultimately, this would cause trust in a network of any type of diminish and would cause people to stop trading on any type of digital platform, including bitcoin. Obviously, this problem is a big one, and bitcoin was ultimately able to counter it by developing blockchain. Let's take a look at some of the details of how blockchain works so that you can better understand how transactions occur in a decentralized and open digital network.

Blockchain 101

The name "blockchain" has to do with the idea that transactions that occur around the same time on a blockchain network are grouped together into blocks. This is how bitcoin solved the problem of having multiple transactions taking place at the same time. Once the transactions that have occurred closely together have been put into blocks, they are then uploaded to the entire network in sequential order and connected to it via a chain system. This is pretty much how the name "blockchain" came to be. These individual transactions that form a block are also transcribed onto the public ledger in a group that contains the following information:

1. The date of the transaction

2. The time of the transaction

3. The participants in the transaction

4. The amount of currency that is being traded between the individuals

Now that the blocks have been constructed, you might be thinking that the problem has been completely solved; however, this is not the case. The creation of the blocks themselves leads to additional problems that must be solved if the blockchain is ever going to run smoothly. Some of these problems include the following: How are these blocks going to get uploaded to the blockchain? Is there any authorization that needs to occur before the blocks are uploaded to the chain? How can it be guaranteed that the people authorizing the transactions are not authorizing fake ones into the system so that they can steal funds? These are all problems that need to be addressed and figured out now that the initial problem has been solved. To begin explaining how all of these problems have been fixed, it's important to first understand the concept of a miner before discussing hash functions, none numbers, and decentralized competition.

Decentralization via a Mining Network

A decentralized network is also known as a Distributed Consensus Model. At this point, you should understand that a decentralized network requires no third-party interaction to verify the trust within a system. Instead, trust is maintained via the network on its own. Decentralization within a Distributed Consensus Model would not be capable without the notion of a miner. A miner is an individual who uses his or her own personal computer in order to police a blockchain network. The essential job of the miner is to construct the blocks that will eventually go into a blockchain, while also collectively agreeing that each transaction is valid and true. Miners are distributed all along a blockchain, and all of them must approve every block of information before it is uploaded to the blockchain. This means that there are multiple people who are looking at a transaction. If information that comes into the network for approval seems sketchy or seems like something is amiss, it is going to have to pass through multiple forms of scrutiny before it is even considered to be uploaded. With more eyes on every transaction, this eliminates the possibility that one miner will be conducting fraudulent activity because he or she is never going to be able to get the block information passed the other miners who are patrolling the network. Of course, these miners do not work for free, at least within the bitcoin network. In exchange for their time and diligence, each miner is provided with a small piece of bitcoin. As you will see in a few moments, the amount of work that a miner has to do certainly warrants compensation of some type.

All About Nodes

Now that you know what a miner is and what these people do within a blockchain system, we can now turn our attention to the concept of nodes. A node can be best defined as anything that is used to facilitate communication within a communication system. Even though we are talking about a digital form of operation when we talk about blockchain, it's important to understand that nodes themselves are considered to be physical in nature. This concept is pretty simple because all it means is that there are physical computers working inside of the blockchain network. The people who are manning these node computers are the miners, the people we were just discussing. This means that when a transaction is completed by two individuals within the network, the node computer receives the information regarding the transaction so that the miner can process it. Every node along the network is receiving the same exact information regarding a transaction, and this ensures that no riffraff can take place within the network. The nodes are verified computers that add yet another layer of protection to the blockchain network so that nothing illegal can occur within its realm.

Now that both the concepts of mining and the concept of physical nodes have been explained, we can now return to the original issue facing bitcoin and blockchain methodology. To refresh your memory, this problem revolved around how to put single transactions into sequential order. While the block method certainly aides in keeping chunks of transactions together in time, there is still another problem that we have to figure out in regards to timing. This problem is figuring out what to do in a situation where two blocks are uploaded to the blockchain at the same time by two different miners. Similar to the idea of multiple transactions taking place at once, this situation may not seem likely to occur, but the reality is that there are many miners working in a blockchain network as fast as they possibly can. With a lot of transactions occurring within the network, there is certainly a need to prioritize blocks as a miner finishes organizing the transactions within them. To figure out this problem, competition between each miner manifested from a mathematical perspective. This will make much more sense after we discuss how hash functions work and what a nonce number is all about.

Competitive Mathematical Calculations

Once a miner has a collection of transactions that have all occurred within the same time period, the block does not simply get added to the chain without any scrutiny or effort. There is still a lot of steps that a miner must take if he or she wants to have the transactions uploaded to the network. The next step for a miner is to complete a series of puzzles to find a nonce number. These puzzles are known as hash functions. These puzzles will typically take a miner around 10 minutes to solve and also will likely require some trial and error math. Let's take a look at the concepts of hash functions and nonce numbers so that you have an idea of how a blockchain network eliminates the possibility that multiple blocks will be uploaded to a blockchain at the same time.

The Basics of Understanding Hash Functions

We have already looked at two examples of cryptographic methods within a blockchain network. These are the public and private keys. It's important to understand that these are not the only two cryptographic methods that exist in a blockchain. Another type of cryptography that is used is known as a hash. A hash is placed along the chain of the blockchain, and this enables multiple security benefits. These benefits include the following:

1. Verify public addresses that exist via the public key

2. Verify the signatures that are being sent via the private key

3. Verify identifiers

These are the fundamental functions that a hash is able to provide a network. At their core, hash functions are used within a blockchain network specifically as a way to provide "proof of work". This means that there is proof that the miners have done the appropriate work to ensure that what is going into a block is valid and true. You can look at this in the following way: the miners are the people who are patrolling the blockchain network, but the hash functions are the digital algorithms that are patrolling the miners. The concept of a hash function is extremely interesting because this type of patrolling is one that takes the place of a "third-party" institution that is verifying any work; however, it's a function that completely eliminates the potential for human error. This notion makes it seem as if a blockchain network is much more secure than a traditional transaction system because there is one less type of error within it about which you have to worry.

As was already stated, the essential quality of a hash function is to provide a proof of work for the miners in the network. A lesser, yet still important, function of the hash is to also enforce a sense of competition within the blockchain network for the miners. By solving the mathematical equations of the hash function as quickly as possible, a miner is able to get his or her block uploaded to the chain faster than the other miners on the network. Coming in first not only provide a sense of accomplishment for the miner in question but also allows the fastest miner to receive a bit more compensation than the other miners who are behind the winner. Let's take a look at the process that the miner has to go through when he or she is attempting to solve a hash function. An explanation of this process will allow you to see in even more detail how a blockchain works in its entirety.

Step 1 in the Mining Process: Sequencing the Individual Transactions

The first step for a miner once he or she has a group of individual transactions that need to be sequentially organized is to get them into the proper order. While this can easily be determined by looking at the exact time when a transaction was completed, there is a certain way that a blockchain would like its transactions ordered. The type of sequencing that a blockchain follows is known as Little Endian number sequencing. Little Endian sequencing allows for seemingly random information to be turned into information that the blockchain network can recognize and use. To do this type of sequencing, the miners sequence the individual transactions from right to left. The most recent transactions begin on the right, and the less recent transactions are processed to the left of the rightmost transaction. Once the miner has put this information into order based on the

Little Endian number sequencing, he or she is ready to move onto the next step.

Step 2 in the Mining Process: Process the Transactions via Two Predetermined Hash Functions

Once the transactions have been ordered using Little Ending number sequencing, the next step is to process this information into two distinct hash functions. It's important to note here that these hash functions may differ depending on the specifics of the blockchain network in which you're working. The two hash functions at which we're going to look in this book are the ones that are used in bitcoin. The purpose of the hash function is twofold. It's used within a blockchain system as a way to figure out which block will be the next in the chain, and this also adds more protection so that no fraudulent activity can occur within the network. For example, a hash function is able to completely prevent a situation where a miner could process a fake block into the network in an attempt to gain funds. At this point, it is pretty obvious that there are multiple layers of security within a blockchain network. This means that if one method of security were to fail, there would be plenty of others waiting to take its place and keep the system secure.

Remember that paper that the creator of blockchain, Nakamoto, published. Within the pages of that publication were two of the hash functions that are essential to the entire blockchain system that helps bitcoin to run. These two hash functions can be found below:

Bitcoin Hash Function 1:

$$\text{Hash256}(d) = \text{SHA} - 256(\text{SHA} - 256(d))$$

Bitcoin Hash Function 2:

$$\text{Hash160}(d) = \text{RIPEMD} - 160(\text{SHA} - 256(d))$$

Obviously, seeing these hash functions won't do much good if the details of each one are not explained to you in detail. For each of these hash functions, the "d" stands for the sequential transactions that the miners have put into order via the Little Ending number sequencing. The "d" is where this chunk of information would go. Next is the SHA variable. This variable is an acronym, and it stands for "Secure Hash Algorithm". There is another variable that can be found in only one of the functions above. This is the RIPEMD variable. RIPEMD stands for "Race Integrity Primitives Evaluation Message Digest". Once the Little Endian number is plugged into the "d" in the equation, the miner is then ready to move onto the next step. This next step requires solving the hash functions and finding the nonce number.

Step 3 in the Mining Process: Finding the Elusive Nonce Number

The last step that the miner will take before uploading his or her block to the blockchain network is to find the nonce number for the hash function. A nonce number is a number that is predefined and only used once. This means that when a miner is looking for a nonce number, this number is going to be a number that he or she has never found while performing math on a hash function before. It's also important to understand that the miner is not just simply figuring out the hash function for the current block that he or she is trying to upload. Instead, the miner is going to figure out the hash function for their current block and then figure out the hash functions for the previous blocks in the blockchain. This means that the miner will be required to do multiple equations, and it is more than likely that he or she is going to have to perform these equations multiple times. On average, it takes a miner about 10 minutes to upload a new block to the blockchain. This mostly has to do with the fact that the miner is figuring out the hash functions for multiple blocks, and it may take a few tries to accurately find this number. You are now aware of the somewhat tedious process that a miner has to go through in order to upload a block to the blockchain. This may make it a bit more obvious as to why a miner gets paid in return for their time working on the network.

This chapter, in conjunction with the previous chapter, should have been able to provide you with information on how a blockchain actually operates. Again, we used the example of bitcoin as our primary point of accessibility for this topic because bitcoin is what started the progression of blockchain to what it is today; however, since bitcoin's introduction blockchain has evolved into technology that can be used in both the financial and non-financial sector alike. These following chapters will document for you how blockchain is being used and where technology gurus are expecting blockchain to be able to take society in the future.

Chapter 4
Blockchain Growth Potential within the Financial Sector

As we have already seen in the first chapter, the Internet has brought people to a point where they want to be able to gamble and place money on societal outcomes; however, many people who are gambling their money on a predictive platform via the Internet are currently doing this without any type of regulation. Of course, it's safe to say that an important goal for the government is to be able to regulate this type of online activity one day, both for the purpose of collecting taxes and other related fees and also ensuring that investor money is safe and secure. It's anticipated that with the help of blockchain technology, there may come a day where a decentralized form of the stock market will be able to exist completely on the Internet. Gone will be the days of a physical Wall Street center. This chapter will look at how blockchain could potentially influence the financial sector of society in the future and will also document the risks that could be associated with this type of decentralized activity for investors and the stock market as a whole.

Becoming a Publicly Traded Company

As it stands right now, it is pretty expensive for any private company to take their company public and have shares of it be traded on the open stock market. In order for this to happen, the company must first meet several criteria. If the company in question is able to meet these requirements, this still does not completely guarantee that the company will be cleared to become a publicly traded company. Below is a list of some of the criteria that a company must meet if and when it is looking to become traded on arguably the most highly regarded stock market, the New York Stock Exchange:

Criteria 1: The company must fill out an application. There are multiple purposes for requiring that an application be filled out, but the biggest one is to make sure that the applicant is willing to adhere to all of the rules that the Exchange has in place.

Criteria 2: The company must fill out a company description. This allows the Exchange to become acquainted with the business that is looking to gain entry into the stock market.

Criteria 3: The company must prove that it already has at least 400 shareholders and that all of these shareholders are holding at least 100 shares of the company. This proves to the New York Stock Exchange that the company already has a lot of investors and that there is little risk to the Exchange to bring this company into its ranks.

Criteria 4: The company must have at least one million dollars that is in the hands of its investors.

Criteria 5: One last criteria that the company in question must meet is that it must prove that it's made at least ten million dollars in the last three consecutive years that it's been in business.

As you can see from the list of criteria above, these requirements certainly narrow down which companies will be able to trade publicly on the New York Stock Exchange. It's also important to understand two additional points. The first point is that there are more than these five criteria that must be met when a company wants to join the New York Stock Exchange (this is a list of the most important ones). The second point is that even if a company does in fact meet all of the necessary criteria to become a publicly traded company, they still may ultimately be denied entry. The Stock Exchange committee may decide that the company in question is ill-suited to be traded in a way that is similar to an auction, for example. This case-by-case system of determining which companies get to trade on the stock market and which companies must sit on the sidelines and watch is a bit subjective to say the least. Blockchain technology could possibly make it easier for more companies to join the stock market in an objective manner. If this is eventually possible, it could drastically change how the stock market operates and what society values from a company from a financial perspective.

An Improved Blockchain-Oriented Exchange

Let's pretend for a minute that the world does come to use blockchain methods to create a digital stock market. How would this stock market operate, and how would it differ from the stock market that we currently know? Firstly, instead of having miners operating the nodes along the blockchain network, these computers would be operated by brokers, who are licensed to conduct trades on the blockchain stock market network. Today, brokers are required to be licensed with the stock market in order to trade on an investor's behalf, so this concept would largely stay intact if we were to adopt a blockchain network. These brokers would be able to collectively verify the validity of stock market transactions that are taking place amongst companies within the network, and they would patrol the blockchain network just as the miners do within bitcoin.

Another important point to make here is that a company who was looking for entry into the stock market would not necessarily have to wait to hear back from a privatized stock market committee as to whether or not their private company is allowed to become publicly traded. Remember that a key factor of any blockchain network is decentralization. There is no small group of millionaires who are working inside of a blockchain network to make sure that only the richest corporations make it into its ranks. Instead, the criteria that a company must meet in order to become publicly traded would be largely mathematical and objective. Once a company is able to prove certain factors about itself, it could upload this information for all of the miners (or in this case, brokers) to review for validity. Once it's been proven that the company has met the qualifications required in order to join the stock market, there would be no subjective waiting period. Decentralization means more accessibility for all of society, and this would help out companies who may otherwise not be admitted into the traditional stock market as we know it today.

The notion of the public ledger would still be similar to the public ledger that was seen within the bitcoin network. A stock exchange ledger would simply detail the trade that was made between a certain company and an individual, the number of shares that was exchanged between the two parties, and the date and time of when the transaction would take place. These entities would still provide their public and private keys to one another, and this again would help to ensure that honesty was being upheld by all members within the stock market network. As you can see, this new stock market network would work similarly to both bitcoin and the traditional stock market, but with some key differences. Adoption of a blockchain-oriented stock market would allow for greater transparency, decentralization, and accessibility for all. Of course, a description of this type of stock market makes it seem quite idealized. Let's take a look at some of the key advantages and disadvantages that would exist if this type of stock market were to be adopted. This way, we will be able to get a clearer picture of whether or not developing this type of stock market would be advantageous or detrimental to society.

Advantages to Blockchain Stock Market Implementation

1. The first advantage to a stock market that revolves around blockchain methodology would be less fraud. As you are probably already aware, there are countless moments in history where big-time stock market investors have gained great reputations as moneymakers, only for the public to ultimately find out that these people were lying and stealing from individuals on the stock market for years. A notorious example of this is the activity of Bernie Madoff. By falsifying account information and lying to the Security and Exchange Commission (SEC), Madoff was able to make it seem as if he was accumulating vast amounts of wealth for his investors. In reality, Madoff was conducting a Ponzi-like scheme to get by. Eventually Madoff was jailed, but not before his investors lost millions of dollars. Some of his investors even killed themselves over the losses that were Madoff's fault.

2. Another advantage that would exist on a blockchain stock market would be the need for less personnel. As it stands now, auditors are employed on the stock market who are there to verify trades between companies and individuals. On a blockchain system, the verification is done via the miners

and the algorithms that are built into the system itself, so there would be less of a need for employees.

3. If there were less employees, this would mean that there would be fewer stock market salaries to pay. This fact could potentially trickle down and make the overall transaction costs of purchasing and trading stocks lower on the stock market. With lower transaction costs, the potential would exist for people to spend more of their money on stock market shares, and this would help to keep the stock market healthily financed for the long term.

4. A stock market backed by block chain would allow for transactions to occur more quickly. While today, the stock market would like to claim that their transactions are processed quickly, this is not always the case. In some parts of the world, it can take up to 3 days for a transaction to finish and the funds to show up in an account. During this waiting period, the stock market is still operating and share prices are changing. If transaction periods were able to happen faster, a person would have the ability to make better decisions with his or her money, without feeling as if he or she is missing out on trading days. The cryptocurrency or proof of ownership of shares would be able to show up in someone's account as soon as the miners have verified that the transaction is valid. This type of speed also allows the individual investor to feel as if he or she is purchasing something with a credit card, instead of "investing" in something wildly significant.

Disadvantages to Blockchain Stock Market Implementation

1. One of the biggest disadvantages that a blockchain stock market currently faces is the idea of the brokers being incentivized for the wrong reasons. For example, miners within the bitcoin network are able to be compensated with bitcoin currency, without much of a problem because these payments are not in competition with one another in anyway. In a stock market system, it's different. If a broker within the stock market system is being paid for their work, the question then becomes how are they being paid? There are many shares from which to choose. Another question concerns the honesty of the broker. If a broker knows that he or she will be paid through a particular stock, does this mean that he or she could potentially manipulate how the shares of the stock are priced so that it works in their favor? If the brokers were to work collaboratively in some way, the result could be complete stock market system corruption.

2. Another huge problem that this type of stock market faces is detrimental transparency. Ideally, transparency is seen as a positive aspect of the blockchain system; however, this is not always with case for people who are trading on the stock market. For example, there is one type of stock market exchange that is known as a super fund. With this type of fund, a huge pot of money is sold over a long period of time, but in a consistent manner. This may mean that twice a week

for 3 months, an investor is predictably spending $10,000 (this is just an example). Obviously, the investor is not going to tell everyone in the stock market that he or she is doing this because if they did, people may manipulate their money in a particular way with this in mind and the price of the stock would change.

In a blockchain system, being able to see this money being spent and manifested on the public ledger could work to the detriment of someone who is using a super fund. The simple fact of the matter is that not all investors are looking for transparency. This is obviously an obstacle that a blockchain stock market would have to overcome in some way shape or form.

From reading this chapter, it should be obvious that the advantages to a digital stock market seem to exceed the disadvantages to developing one; however, this does not mean that there are not still obstacles to overcome before this type of network even comes close to being developed. The traditional stock market as we know it today was not developed overnight, and there is no way that a stock market built on a blockchain network would be built any faster. There are many factors to consider when developing any new type of global technology, but seeing the capabilities and the limitations of this type of mechanism should get you excited about the future of our financial networks over the long term.

Chapter 5

Blockchain Potential in the Non-Financial Sector

Now that we have looked a major way that blockchain could potentially be used in the financial sector through stock market implementation, it's time to look at the ways that blockchain could influence non-financial institutions. Before we dive into this chapter and look at any specific ways the blockchain can influence the non-financial sector, it's important to take a step back and look at a key element of blockchain. Even though so far, we have only talked about blockchain from the perspective of currency exchange, the prowess of blockchain has to do more with defining ownership than anything else. Blockchain is able to organize who owns what and when, while also being able to provide information on who owned what previously and how much of it was owned. This idea of ownership is where the non-financial aspects of blockchain potential is headed. This chapter will look at what Ethereum and Smart Contracts are and how these applications are both using blockchain as a way to prove individual ownership within their respective networks.

Build Your Own Blockchain with the Help of Ethereum

Ethereum is an open-source network that seems to have taken the basic points of the bitcoin application and expanded on them. Within Ethereum, you're able to build your own blockchain database. A key feature of Ethereum is the fact that you are able to trade internationally on its platform, via its EVM. EVM stands for Ethereum Virtual Machine. If you were to decide that you wanted to build your own blockchain platform using Ethereum, here is a list of some of the things you could do:

1. Create your own currency. The currency that is inherent to Ethereum is known as Ether; however, once you open up your own blockchain network on the Ethereum platform, you have the ability to create a currency that is completely unique to your blockchain network.

2. Operate your own market. Let's say that you sell your own products on the Internet. A blockchain network would allow you to completely centralize your product and develop an online marketplace for yourself that does not require dependence on Amazon or another super corporation. You would be completely in charge of how your market is run.

3. Keep track of where your money is going. Your blockchain network on the Ethereum platform would

allow you to keep track of the debts that people owe you along with your profitability.

4. Although we will get to what Smart Contracts are later in this chapter, Ethereum also allows you to develop contracts with people on your network. This allows you to prove who owns what.

5. Ethereum also allows their users to process ownership in the case of death. This includes the fulfillment of wills or other types of death documents where ownership needs to be processed to someone else.

As you can see, Ethereum has been developed to go beyond the capabilities of a single bitcoin system. You can think of Ethereum as being able to provide you with the capability to start your own digital marketplace. Instead of subscribing to an already operational network (such as what you do on a platform such as Etsy or eBay), you are truly calling the shots and controlling your interaction with your customers. This is a real consumer innovation that would not be possible without the Internet or blockchain methodology. The Ethereum application makes it pretty clear that society has not reached its full blockchain potential.

Declaring Ownership with Smart Contracts

At its core, the application of the Smart Contract allows people to trade ownership of goods or services without having to meet in person. This concept was developed by the developed Nick Szabo. At first, this concept may not seem like it would be particularly beneficial, but you may change your mind after it's put into perspective a bit. For example, if you have ever tried to purchase a home before, you already know that there are many aspects to the home buying process. When you purchase a home, you have to contact your bank, a mortgage lender, a realtor, a lawyer, and the selling agent as well. You also need a home inspector and potentially other types of people such as mold removal experts or asbestos removal experts. It's safe to say that this process can become complex quickly. If you're unorganized, the potential for a headache of a time is pretty high.

These complicated processes are the types of circumstances that the notion of a Smart Contract seeks to rectify. It uses blockchain technology to allow multiple enterprises to see the progress of contract completion, as long as access is granted to these different entities. Another way to think about how a Smart Contract works is to consider it as being similar to a checklist. Let's take the example of buying a house. When you buy a house, just a few of the documents that you will need to verify and present on the day of closing include down payment amount, any completion items that the seller has agreed to rectify for you, and documents that a lawyer will need you to sign to make the sale final. When these items are online and in a digital format, all of the parties who are involved in the home buying transaction are able to see the progress of these documents. Additionally, the seller and the buyer are able to sign their documents electronically, and a need for a sit-down meeting becomes obsolete. Smart Contracts allow for virtual roundtable interaction. This saves the entire process time and makes the entire home buying process easier for everyone involved.

If we go beyond the example of buying a home, it is also possible to see how a Smart Contract is largely more efficient than a traditional contract. For example, let's take the example renting an apartment. Let's say that you are a landlord. You're also rich, and you decide that you're going to spend your money by purchasing an apartment complex that can hold 20 residents. Obviously, managing 20 homes is going to be considerable work for you, especially when rent day comes. A primary goal of a landlord is to get paid on time, yet so often, it seems as if a rent payment is late and the landlord is the one who has to carry the burden of this late payment. Of course, almost every rent contract has a stipulation in it regarding an additional cost that is accrued when a rent payment is late, but this late fee is not always tacked onto the cost of rent for the month. We can all agree that this is a problem, especially for a landlord who needs to make ends meet each month.

A Smart Contract takes some of the responsibility of having to pester people for their rent payments from the landlord and places back on itself. If you were a landlord and decided to organize your individual leases using a Smart Contract network, this would mean that the Smart Contract would be automatically be able to determine when a tenant's rent was late. It would automatically be able to generate a late fee to the tenant's wallet as soon as the 1st of the month came and went, alleviating pressure from the landlord to track down the tenant and demand payment. With a Smart Contract, the algorithms that are built into the network use "if", "and", and "or" statements in order to figure out when certain stipulations need to occur. The Smart Contract keeps tabs on the state of contract compliance. If a portion of the contract is violated, the Smart Contract takes immediate action.

The Advantages of Using a Smart Contract

Currently, there are a variety of advantages that are available to someone who opts to become a part of a Smart Contract network. One of these advantages is the idea that you are now able to combine Smart Contracts with use on your own Ethereum network if you wish to do so. Doing this allows you to make your Ethereum network even more efficient, depending on the venture or marketplace that you're trying to operate while using it. Let's take a look at some of the advantages that using a Smart Contract can provide an individual so that it's even more obvious as to why the future of all contractual obligations may take place using this type of digital ownership.

Advantage 1: More Efficient Transparency

If we go back to the example of the landlord using the Smart Contract system to make sure that he or she is getting paid on time, it is obvious that the Smart Contract is able to provide both the landlord and the tenant with optimum informational insight. Sticking to the notion of the public ledger but adapting it a bit, the Smart Contract allows visibility of the contract to be seen between both the tenant and the landlord. All members of any type of contract are able to interact with the contract together, and this makes accessibility of the contract easier for all of the parties who are involved. If the landlord of an apartment complex were to charge a late fee to a tenant's account, this late fee would immediately show on the contract ledger. The tenant would have no questions as to why they were charged more money, and it would be hard to dispute this charge when the explanation is as clear as day. The Smart Contract is able to optimize the idea of transparency, while keeping all aspects of a contract organized and succinct.

Advantage 2: Maintain Obligation

People get sued all of the time for a variety of reasons. One reason out of many is because of the fact that not everyone stays true to a contract that they initially sign. A Smart Contract makes it harder for someone to break a contract because of the fact that this type of contract is going to be tied to an individual's online presence. For example, it's likely that you are constantly bombarded with emails on the regular. Even if you don't like receiving the emails that are asking you to sign up for this or purchase that, it's almost impossible to completely rid yourself of this type of relentless advertising. With notifications that happen on a Smart Contract being directly connected to your identity within a computer, it will be easier than ever for a person with whom you're engaged in a contract to contact you or seek you out when you are in violation of something. This idea makes it obvious that the entire way in which people maintain their obligations to one another could change if Smart Contracts ever end up becoming popular or even replacing the traditional method of how contracts are kept. Remember, none of these considerations would be possible without the notion of the blockchain.

While the two main advantages to using Smart Contracts have been stated above, one disadvantage that still needs to be worked out includes keeping a contract private when needed. Most blockchain networks are transparent by nature; yet, it should be obvious that there are instances when a company may want to keep their business private for one reason or another. The kinks that surround the idea of privacy within a Smart Contract network are still being discussed; however, it should be apparent that this same problem keeps popping up in our blockchain examples.

Remember the chapter that described the blockchain stock market. The same problem regarding the super fund occurred in that network as well. The discussion of how much transparency is a good thing is one that may not have a solid or black-and-white answer. It's also not a question that will have the same answering, depending on who you ask. The amount of transparency that a marketplace should ideally have is an ethical question that has no "right" answer. This is why it's important that you as an individual keep an eye on how blockchain developers are answering this question.

Chapter 6
Implications for the Future of Blockchain Technology

At this point in the book, it should be obvious that blockchain technology has the potential to completely revolutionize the way in which people and all of humanity interacts with their physical surroundings and infrastructures. The thought that one day you could potentially operate within a digital nation or digital town square has finally come to fruition, and its origins live in what blockchain has to offer. This chapter will look at the future of blockchain and how this type of technology could possibly be the wave of the future for many years to come from a technological and digital perspective.

Fintech and Its Future

Fintech is an abbreviated word that stands for "Financial Technology". We have already looked an example of fintech through our discussion of a blockchain platform that helps to operate the stock market, but there are many other networks that are out there that are both already developed and in the process of being developed. It's pretty easy to understand why fintech concepts would be important to banking institutions all over the world. No large banking corporation wants to become obsolete due to digital financial advancements, which is why so many of these institutions have already started to develop their own blockchain operational networks. For example, mega-corporations such as Goldman Sachs and IBM have put a lot of money into developing blockchain networks from which their banks can operate. These banks hope that if and when blockchain technology takes over, their institutions will be safe from complete obliteration into nonexistence.

It's safe to say that there are two other reasons why banks have a large interest in developing blockchain networks of their own. The first reason has to do with trust. Obviously, trustworthiness is an essential quality that any bank must prove that they have to the public if they ever hope to have a lot of business. These days, people are more skeptical than ever before, and not everyone trusts the idea that a private bank is going to manage their money with the most altruistic interests in mind. Often, individuals within a privatized bank will act secretly selfish, in the hope that they will be able to yield higher dividends of profit. Along this line of thinking, if a big bank was able to say that they are now operating on a decentralized and transparent network, then this could make less of the public less skeptical about their operations and, thus, the bank could acquire more business for itself.

The second reason why a bank might have a vested interest in developing a blockchain network is because they can still potentially maintain privatization on the network, even though they are outwardly claiming that their network is open source. If everyone on the blockchain system that is owned by a bank works for the bank, then how is the idea of transparency truly maintained? This idea makes it necessary to step back and think about the implications of doing business with a bank that has been developed on a blockchain network. Unless you as an individual are able to log into the bank's blockchain network and see a public ledger of your fund activity for yourself, transparency as an ideal has been manipulated by the banks to be something that is less transparent and more controlled than is truly necessary on a blockchain network.

Blockchain and Use in the Government

As of February 2017, there was only one country that has taken concrete steps (so far) towards using blockchain technology in any serious way within society. This country was the Republic of Georgia. They approved legislation which stated that blockchain technology could be used as a way to prove ownership of land within its country's borders. Specifically, blockchain technology will now be used to authorize new land titles, trade ownership of land between people who are looking to buy and sell property, approve a situation where people are looking to demolish property that is on their own land, and provide services related to mortgage lending and housing endeavors. The Republic of Georgia is the first country to legally authorize the use of blockchain within its society, but it is safe to say that they will not be the last. Honduras and Sweden, just to name two, have also begun looking into how they can use blockchain within their respective societies.

The Future of Blockchain

The fact that an actual government has authorized the use of blockchain for municipal decisions in a society should be ultimate proof to you that blockchain is going to definitely have concrete influence in our world. If we think creatively for a minute, the potential for how our society could be influenced by blockchain is vast and complex. Of course, there are plenty of questions that come with this type of digital development, but these questions will surely be answered in time if blockchain technology is ever going to be considered a viable tool for the proof of ownership. As of right now, the potential for blockchain technology seems endless.

Even though the potential for blockchain seems endless, it is doubly important that society recognizes the great risks that come along with developing new types of technology and ways of currency exchange. Intrade.com, for example, did not adequately prepare itself for the speed at which their company would grow. This ultimately led to many people losing their money. The major risks that are currently associated with blockchain include questions regarding how insurance companies will operate within it, how currency will be valued properly, and how it can be regulated by the government. These important questions require that developers work both diligently and carefully to provide society with technology that is even safer than the physical institutions that are currently the pillars of how our societies operate.

Conclusion

Thanks for making it through to the end of *Blockchain: How the Technology Behind Bitcoin Is Changing Money and Business.* Hopefully, this book has been able to provide you with diverse and useful information on the topic of blockchain technology. Obviously, the basics of blockchain technology can be a bit complicated; however, these complicated processes can more easily be explained through how the bitcoin operating system works and what it's all about. The biggest takeaway from this book that's important to understand about blockchain in general is that its primary usefulness to the world is that it can help to verify ownership of all types. Even though this book spent a lot of time discussing blockchain from a financial perspective, there are plenty of non-financial endeavors that are also being capitalized upon through the means of the blockchain. This makes the future of blockchain capabilities large because it is able to influence society from multiple angles.

The next step is to continue doing research about blockchain. While this book was able to provide you with details about applications that are currently using blockchain to create a transparent and efficient digital environment, such as Ethereum and Smart Contracts, there are plenty of other blockchain systems that are already on the market and have yet to be created. For example, did you know the services such as Venmo, Airbnb, and even Netflix are currently using blockchain tactics to some extent in order to operate? Since it is obvious that blockchain is not going anywhere anytime soon, it's important that you are ahead of the curve and understand the implications of this technology to the fullest extent possible. Even though this book has discussed a large chunk of how blockchain can possibly change our global society, it's still possible that unanticipated aspects of blockchain have yet to be discovered. That's what makes the future of blockchain society exciting and why you should care about where this technology can take us.

Finally, if you found this book useful in any way, a review on Amazon is always appreciated!

Do you have any feedback or typo to report?

Email me at bresettmark@gmail.com.

Printed in Great Britain
by Amazon